God Created Me Too

written by Dot Cachiaras

illustrated by Kay Salem

for Kristen

Library of Congress Catalog Card No. 86-63566
© 1987. The STANDARD PUBLISHING Company, Cincinnati, Ohio
Division of STANDEX INTERNATIONAL Corporation. Printed in U.S.A.

It seems to me
  Since God made the moon
  And all of the stars, twinkling bright . . .

Then surely my God
  Created me too,
    And touched me with His special light.

It seems to me
    Since God made the trees
    To grow on the earth with green leaves . . .

Then surely my God
Created me too,
To stretch up toward Him when I please.

It seems to me
  Since God made the sands
  And the blue seas lapping the shore . . .

Then surely my God
  Created me too,
  And touches my life even more.

It seems to me
Since God made the sky
To cover the earth and the sea . . .

Then surely my God
    Created me too,
And that's why I look
JUST LIKE ME!

It seems to me
　Since God made the birds
　　To fly through His beautiful sky . . .

Then surely my God
Created me too,
To live with Him someday on high.

It seems to me
  Since God made the flowers
  To grow and to nod and to sway . . .

Then surely my God
Created me too,
To look up to Him everyday.

It seems to me
Since God made the grass,
So shiny and spikey and green . . .

Then surely my God
Created me too
So my smile could
brighten the scene.

It seems to me
Since God made the fish
To swim in the depths of the sea . . .

Then surely my God
Created me too
To swim and to splash blissfully!

It seems to me
Since God made the rain
To fall on the earth everywhere ...

Then surely my God
  Created me too,
  And keeps me in His love and care.

It seems to me
Since God made the ducks,
The elephants, monkeys and deer . . .

Then surely my God
   Created me too,
And I trust Him
   to always stay near.

It seems to me
   Since God made the night
   And warm, sunny hours we call day . . .

Then surely my God
  Created me too
  To thank Him with love when I pray.

"Thank You, dear God,
for creating me too!"